Rookie
Read-About®
Health

WITHDRAWN

I Have a Cold

by Lisa M. Herrington

Content Consultant
Catherine A. Dennis, N.P.

Reading Consultant
Jeanne M. Clidas, Ph.
Reading Specialist

Children's Press®
An Imprint of Scholastic I
New York Toronto London Auckla
Mexico City New Delhi Hong Kong
Danbury, Connecticut

Library of Congress Cataloging-in-Publication Data
Herrington, Lisa M.
 I have a cold/by Lisa M. Herrington.
     pages cm. — (Rookie read-about health).
Audience: Ages 3-6
Includes bibliographical references and index.
 ISBN 978-0-531-21012-3 (library binding: alk. paper) — ISBN 978-0-531-21069-7
(pbk.: alk. paper)
1. Cold (Disease)—Juvenile literature. 2. Bacteria—Juvenile literature. I. Title. II.
Series: Rookie read-about health.

 RF361.H47 2015
 616.2'05—dc23   2014035908

Produced by Spooky Cheetah Press
Design by Keith Plechaty

Printed in China 62

SCHOLASTIC, CHILDREN'S PRESS, ROOKIE READ-ABOUT®, and associated logos
are trademarks and/or registered trademarks of Scholastic Inc.

1 2 3 4 5 6 7 8 9 10 R 24 23 22 21 20 19 18 17 16 15

Photographs ©: Getty Images/2A Images: 23, 29 bottom right; iStockphoto: 30, 31
center top (aabejon), 27 bottom, 31 top (bonniej), 20 (killerb10), 4, 31 center bottom
(princessdlaf); Media Bakery: 12, 19, 27 top right, 29 top left (KidStock), 28 (Sander),
8 main (Spyros Bourboulis), 6 (Tim Hawley); Newscom/BSIP: 24; Shutterstock, Inc.:
29 bottom left (bikeriderlondon), 27 top left (Hung Chung Chih), 7 (Jamie Wilson),
11, 31 bottom (mathagraphics), 3 top right (Matt Antonino), cover (reporter), 3 top
left (victoriaKh); Superstock, Inc./LEMOINE/BSIP: 29 top right; Thinkstock: 8 inset
(IPGGutenbergUKLtd), 3 bottom (Mega_Pixel), 15 (monkeybusinessimages).

Table of Contents

Get Well Soon!

Your nose is runny. You have a sore throat. Your head feels stuffy. You keep sneezing and coughing. You probably have a cold!

Sooner or later, we all catch colds. Kids get about six to ten colds a year. A cold usually lasts about a week. Hang in there, though. You will feel better soon.

FAST FACT!

Colds are one of the top reasons that kids miss school.

Germs can enter the body through the nose.

Tiny hairs inside the nose stop many germs.

A sneeze can travel as fast as a train. It blasts germs out of the body.

8

What Is a Cold?

A cold is a mild illness. It mainly affects your nose and throat.

When you breathe, tiny germs can enter your body through your nose. Tiny hairs inside your nose may keep germs from going farther into your body.

Tiny viruses can only be seen with strong microscopes.

Every so often, some germs make it into your body. A **virus** is a germ. There are more than 200 viruses that can cause colds. Your **immune system** works hard to fight them.

FAST FACT!

You cannot catch a cold from going outside in chilly weather.

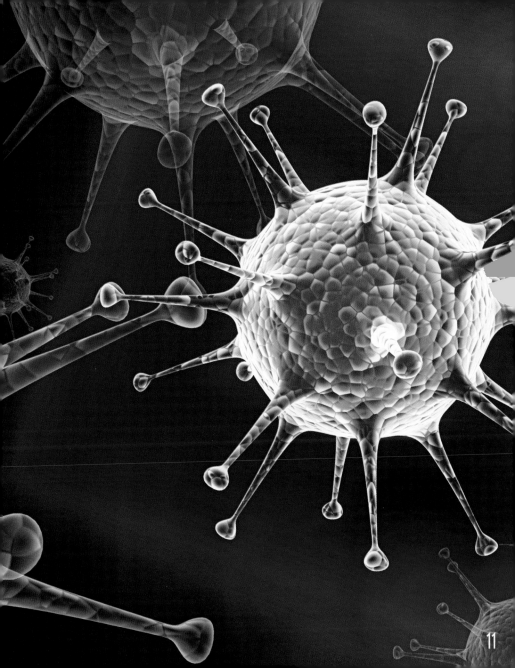

Cold viruses spread easily. They travel through tiny drops of **mucus** in the air. Mucus is wet, slimy fluid in your nose, mouth, and throat. The droplets spray out when someone sneezes or coughs. One way a cold can spread is if you breathe in the droplets.

Colds spread quickly in school because kids are in close contact.

Cold viruses can live on surfaces such as toys, computer keyboards, and doorknobs. You can get sick if you touch a surface with a cold virus on it. The virus can pass to you if you touch your eyes, nose, or mouth.

FAST FACT!

A cold appears about two to three days after you contract a cold virus.

How do you know if you have a cold? **Symptoms** are signs that tell you if you are sick.

Some cold symptoms include:
- runny or stuffy nose
- sore throat
- coughing and sneezing
- feeling tired and not hungry
- low fever

Treating a Cold

There is no cure for a cold, but you can treat it. Your body loses fluids when you are sick. To feel better, drink lots of water. Get plenty of rest, too. An adult may give you medicine to relieve your cough or aches.

Medicine does not make your cold go away faster, but it can help you feel better.

Hot soup and drinks can soothe a sore throat. The heat helps clear the mucus in your throat. Blowing your nose also gets rid of mucus.

FAST FACT!

People always said eating homemade chicken soup helped with a cold. Now scientists have discovered it's true!

Preventing a Cold

Cold germs stick to hands. They can be passed along when you touch another person. Wash your hands with soap and water often. It is the best way to protect yourself from germs.

FAST FACT!

Scrub your hands for at least 20 seconds. That is the time it takes to sing the ABC song!

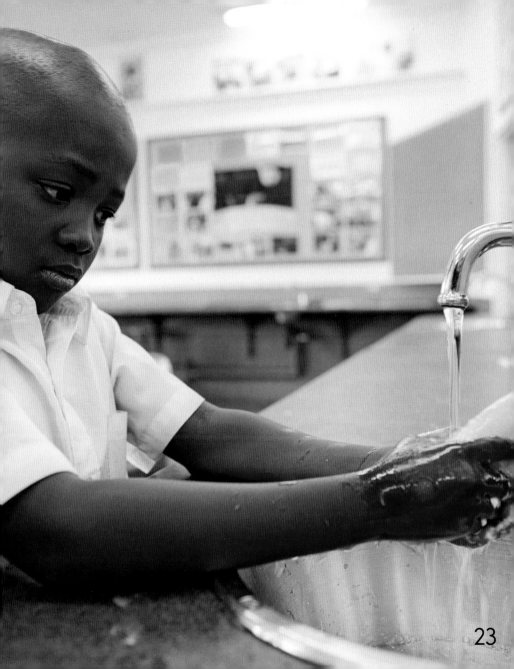

There are other ways to lower your chance of catching a cold:

- Do not share food and drinks with others.
- Stay away from people who are sick.

To keep from getting others sick:

- Cough or sneeze into a tissue.
- Cough or sneeze into your elbow or sleeve instead of your hands.

Taking care of yourself can also help protect you against colds. Eat healthy foods, exercise regularly, and get plenty of sleep. These healthy habits will keep your body strong.

Healthy habits build your immune system so it can fight colds.

Your Turn

How Germs Spread

Find out why it is important to wash your hands.

What You Need: glitter (to represent germs), hand lotion, a paper plate, paper towels, soap, water, a family member

1. Pour a little glitter on the paper plate. Rub a small amount of lotion on your hands. Then place your hands on the glitter. Shake hands with a family member. Notice how the "germs" spread to that person's hand.

2. Wipe your hands with a paper towel. Have your family member do the same. Observe how many of the germs are still on your hands.

3. Scrub your hands with soap and water. Have your family member do the same. Most, if not all, of the germs should be gone.

Healthy Habits

Look at the photos below. Which ones show the best ways to keep cold germs from spreading?

Answers: 1., 4. Coughing into your sleeve and washing your hands help keep germs from spreading.

Strange but True!

Yuck! Slimy mucus may be gross, but it is good for you. Mucus traps germs so they do not enter your body. Your nose makes even more mucus when you catch a cold. This keeps the virus away from other parts of your body. Mucus can come out of your nose. It can also run down your throat.

Just for Fun

Q: Did you hear the story about the germ?

A: Never mind. I don't want to spread it.

Q: How can you make a tissue dance?

A: Put some boogie in it!

Glossary

immune system (i-MYOON SISS-tum): parts of the body that protect you from sickness

mucus (MYOO-kuss): slimy fluid that coats and protects your breathing passages

symptoms (SIMP-tuhms): signs that show you have an illness

virus (VY-russ): tiny type of germ that causes illnesses, such as a cold

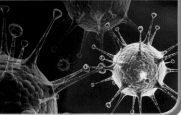

Index

Facts for Now

Visit this Scholastic Web site for more information on colds:
www.factsfornow.scholastic.com
Enter the keyword **Colds**

About the Author

Lisa M. Herrington enjoys writing books and articles for kids. She lives in Trumbull, Connecticut, with her husband, Ryan, and daughter, Caroline. Lisa likes to drink tea when she feels under the weather.